Beatrix Potter

Beatrix Potter
99 Cliparts Book Part 2

13_Cliparts_Patty_pan.png

by
Elizabeth M. Potter

Content	Page

99 Cliparts

I.	The Tale of Tom Kitten	3
II.	The Tale of Samuel Whiskers	6
III.	The Tailor of Gloucester	9
IV.	The Tale of the Pie and the Patty-Pan	11
V.	The Sly Old Cat	14
VI.	The Story of Miss Moppet	16
VII.	The Fox and the Stork	18
VIII.	Three little mice	19

16 Bonus Cliparts

I.	The Tale of Mrs. Tiggy-Winkle	20

Instructions for downloading the Cliparts	23
Further books of Elizabeth M. Potter	24

Bibliografische Information der Deutschen Nationalbibliothek:
Die Deutsche Nationalbibliothek verzeichnet diese Publikation in der Deutschen Nationalbibliografie; detaillierte bibliografische
Daten sind im Internet über http://dnb.dnb.de abrufbar.

© 2018 Elizabeth M. Potter 1. Auflage
Covergrafik, Texte und Bilder: © 2018 Elizabeth M. Potter

Herstellung und Verlag: BoD – Books on Demand, Norderstedt

ISBN: 9783752867084

The Tale of Tom Kitten

1_Cliparts_Tom_Kitten.png

2_Cliparts_Tom_Kitten.png

3_Cliparts_Tom_Kitten.png

4_Cliparts_Tom_Kitten.png

5_Cliparts_Tom_Kitten.png

6_Cliparts_Tom_Kitten.png

7_Cliparts_Tom_Kitten.png

8_Cliparts_Tom_Kitten.png

9_Cliparts_Tom_Kitten.png

10_Cliparts_Tom_Kitten.png

11_Cliparts_Tom_Kitten.png

12_Cliparts_Tom_Kitten.png

4

13_Cliparts_Tom_Kitten.png

14_Cliparts_Tom_Kitten.png

15_Cliparts_Tom_Kitten.png

16_Cliparts_Tom_Kitten.png

The Tale of Samuel Whiskers

1_Cliparts_Whiskers.png

2_Cliparts_Whiskers.png

3_Cliparts_Whiskers.png

4_Cliparts_Whiskers.png

5_Cliparts_Whiskers.png

6_Cliparts_Whiskers.png

7_Cliparts_Whiskers.png

8_Cliparts_Whiskers.png

9_Cliparts_Whiskers.png

10_Cliparts_Whiskers.png

11_Cliparts_Whiskers.png

12_Cliparts_Whiskers.png

13_Cliparts_Whiskers.png

14_Cliparts_Whiskers.png

15_Cliparts_Whiskers.png

16_Cliparts_Whiskers.png

17_Cliparts_Whiskers.png

18_Cliparts_Whiskers.png

19_Cliparts_Whiskers.png

20_Cliparts_Whiskers.png

21_Cliparts_Whiskers.png

The Tailor of Gloucester

1_Cliparts_Gloucester.png

2_Cliparts_Gloucester.png

3_Cliparts_Gloucester.png

4_Cliparts_Gloucester.png

5_Cliparts_Gloucester.png

6_Cliparts_Gloucester.png

7_Cliparts_Gloucester.png

8_Cliparts_Gloucester.png

9_Cliparts_Gloucester.png

10_Cliparts_Gloucester.png

11_Cliparts_Gloucester.png

The Tale of the Pie and the Patty-Pan

1_Cliparts_Patty_pan.png

2_Cliparts_Patty_pan.png

3_Cliparts_Patty_pan.png

4_Cliparts_Patty_pan.png

5_Cliparts_Patty_pan.png

6_Cliparts_Patty_pan.png

7_Cliparts_Patty_pan.png

8_Cliparts_Patty_pan.png

9_Cliparts_Patty_pan.png

10_Cliparts_Patty_pan.png

11_Cliparts_Patty_pan.png

12_Cliparts_Patty_pan.png

13_Cliparts_Patty_pan.png

14_Cliparts_Patty_pan.png

15_Cliparts_Patty_pan.png

16_Cliparts_Patty_pan.png

17_Cliparts_Patty_pan.png

18_Cliparts_Patty_pan.png

19_Cliparts_Patty_pan.png

20_Cliparts_Patty_pan.png

The Sly Old Cat

1_Cliparts_Sly_Cat.png

2_Cliparts_Sly_Cat.png

3_Cliparts_Sly_Cat.png

4_Cliparts_Sly_Cat.png

5_Cliparts_Sly_Cat.png

6_Cliparts_Sly_Cat.png

7_Cliparts_Sly_Cat.png

8_Cliparts_Sly_Cat.png

9_Cliparts_Sly_Cat.png

10_Cliparts_Sly_Cat.png

11_Cliparts_Sly_Cat.png

12_Cliparts_Sly_Cat.png

13_Cliparts_Sly_Cat.png

14_Cliparts_Sly_Cat.png

15_Cliparts_Sly_Cat.png

The Story of Miss Moppet

1_Cliparts_Moppet.png

2_Cliparts_Moppet.png

3_Cliparts_Moppet.png

4_Cliparts_Moppet.png

5_Cliparts_Moppet.png

6_Cliparts_Moppet.png

7_Cliparts_Moppet.png

8_Cliparts_Moppet.png

2nd Part of link: **AAC0jDbbnpn-16kaeWoSNTjLa?dl=0**

The Fox and the Stork

1_Cliparts_Stork.png

2_Cliparts_Stork.png

3_Cliparts_Stork.png

4_Cliparts_Stork.png

5_Cliparts_Stork.png

Three little mice

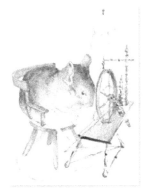

1_Cliparts_Three_little_mice.png

2_Cliparts_Three_little_mice.png

3_Cliparts_Three_little_mice.png

4_Cliparts_Three_little_mice.png

5_Cliparts_Three_little_mice.png

The Tale of Mrs. Tiggy-Winkle

1_Cliparts_Tiggy_Winkle.png

2_Cliparts_Tiggy_Winkle.png

3_Cliparts_Tiggy_Winkle.png

4_Cliparts_Tiggy_Winkle.png

5_Cliparts_Tiggy_Winkle.png

6_Cliparts_Tiggy_Winkle.png

7_Cliparts_Tiggy_Winkle.png

8_Cliparts_Tiggy_Winkle.png

9_Cliparts_Tiggy_Winkle.png

10_Cliparts_Tiggy_Winkle.png

11_Cliparts_Tiggy_Winkle.png

12_Cliparts_Tiggy_Winkle.png

13_Cliparts_Tiggy_Winkle.png

14_Cliparts_Tiggy_Winkle.png

15_Cliparts_Tiggy_Winkle.png

16_Cliparts_Tiggy_Winkle.png

22

Instructions for downloading the Cliparts

Before you are reading the instructions to download/using the cliparts, please read the following handling instructions for the correct usage of the cliparts.

Handling instruction for the usage of the cliparts

The cliparts were created by Elizabeth M. Potter. Therefore please take into account the following before starting the download:

You can use the cliparts for any of your private enterprises, projects, presentations, invitations or the like.
But it is not allowed to use them for commercial purpurses.
If you intend to use them for commercial purpurses, please ask for written approval by Elizabeth M. Potter in advance (elizabeth.potter@t-online.de).
In that case, publishing, republishing or reproductions of the cliparts, especially of the download link, via any kind of service, Internet or graphic service wether as a book, electronically, or via other not listed above media or other means, without prior approval by Elizabeth M. Potter is strongly prohibited.

Clipart download instructions

The cliparts are in a directory of dropbox Service. It is a simple access by typing in the download link into your internet browser. The access is possible via PC, smartphone or tablet. The clipart files are presented in png-format.
For security reasons the link is divided into two parts. For gaining the complete link, both parts have to be typed into the address field of the browser one after another without spaces in between.

1st Part of link: **https://www.dropbox.com/sh/eptqcq70x4ojklc/**
2nd Part of link: you will find on page 17 of this book

Further books of Elizabeth M. Potter

NOTEBOOKS
The Peter Rabbit Notebook
PAINTING BOOKS
Beatrix Potter Painting Book Part 1 (Peter Rabbit)
Beatrix Potter Painting Book Part 2 (Peter Rabbit)
Beatrix Potter Painting Book Part 3 (Peter Rabbit)
Beatrix Potter Painting Book Part 4 (Peter Rabbit)
Beatrix Potter Painting Book Part 5 (Peter Rabbit)
Beatrix Potter Painting Book Part 6 (Peter Rabbit)
Beatrix Potter Painting Book Part 7 (Peter Rabbit)
Beatrix Potter Painting Book Part 8 (Peter Rabbit)
Beatrix Potter Painting Book Part 9 (Peter Rabbit)
Beatrix Potter Painting Book Part 10 (Peter Rabbit)
Peter Rabbit Painting Book
CLIPART BOOKS
Beatrix Potter 99 Cliparts Book Part 1 (Peter Rabbit)
Beatrix Potter 99 Cliparts Book Part 2 (Peter Rabbit)
Beatrix Potter 99 Cliparts Book Part 3 (Peter Rabbit)
Beatrix Potter 99 Cliparts Book Part 4 (Peter Rabbit)
PASSWORD BOOKS
The Peter Rabbit Passwortbook